Healing from Infidelity

A Comprehensive book guide to Rebuilding Trust in your Marriage & relationship, and sudden heartbreak affair caused by your partner…

By

Mildred Kent

TABLE OF CONTENTS

CHAPTER ONE..**9**

Understanding Infidelity...........................**9**

   1.1 **Defining Infidelity under Types and Forms**.. 9

   1.2 **Exploring the Reasons Behind Infidelity**... 10

   1.3 **Recognizing the Emotional Impact on the Betrayed Partner**................................. 12

CHAPTER TWO.. 15

Coping with Betrayal................................. 15

   2.1 **Processing Shock and Disbelief under Betrayal**.. 15

   2.2 **Managing Intense Emotions: Anger, Hurt, and Sadness under Betrayal**............... 16

   2.3 **Seeking Support: Friends, Family, and Professionals**....................................17

CHAPTER THREE... 19

Rebuilding Trust under Infidelity.................. 19

   3.1 **The Importance of Transparency and Honesty under Relationships**...................... 20

   3.2 **Setting Boundaries and Expectations under Relationships**.................................20

   3.3 **Strategies for Restoring Trust in the Relationship**..21

CHAPTER FOUR..25

Communicating Effectively.............................25

    4.1 **Opening Up Dialogue About Feelings and Concerns**..25

    4.2 **Active Listening and Validation**..........26

    4.3 **Resolving Conflict Constructively**......27

CHAPTER FIVE...29

Forgiveness and Moving Forward.....................29

    5.1 **Understanding the Process of Forgiveness**...29

    5.2 **Letting Go of Resentment and Bitterness**..31

    5.3 **Embracing Healing and Growth Opportunities**..32

CHAPTER SIX...35

Reconnecting Intimately After Infidelity in Relationships..35

    6.1 **Rebuilding Emotional Intimacy**..........35

    6.2 **Restoring Physical Intimacy and Affection**...37

    6.3 **Overcoming Challenges and Barriers to Reconnection**...38

CHAPTER SEVEN...41

Addressing Underlying Issues Under Infidelity Relationships..41

    7.1 **Exploring Contributing Factors: Stress, Communication, etc.**.....................................42

    7.2 **Healing Past Wounds and Trauma**....43

    7.3 **Seeking Professional Help: Therapy and Counseling**..44

CHAPTER EIGHT..**47**

Strengthening the Relationship.........................**47**

    8.1 **Cultivating Friendship and Mutual Respect**.. 48

    8.2 **Fostering a Culture of Appreciation and Gratitude**...49

    8.3 **Investing in the Relationship: Quality Time and Shared Goals**............................. 50

CHAPTER NINE...**53**

Managing Triggers and Relapses.....................**53**

    9.1 **Identifying Triggers That Reignite Pain and Doubt**...53

    9.2 **Developing Coping Strategies and Self-Care Practices**..................................... 54

    9.3 **Reaffirming Commitment and Resilience in the Face of Setbacks**................................55

CHAPTER TEN..**59**

Embracing a New Beginning After the Phase of Infidelity in Relationship...................................**59**

    10.1 **Reclaiming Personal Identity and Confidence**.. 60

    10.2 **Building a Shared Vision for the Future**.. 61

    10.3 **Celebrating Milestones and Achievements in the Healing Journey***........ 62

    10.4 **Questions and Discussion under Healing from Infidelity**....................................63

CHAPTER ONE

Understanding Infidelity

Infidelity, often considered one of the most painful betrayals in a relationship, is the act of engaging in romantic or sexual activities outside the agreed-upon boundaries of a committed

partnership. It shatters trust, undermines the foundation of the relationship, and can have profound emotional consequences for both parties involved. Understanding the complexities surrounding infidelity requires delving into its various types, forms, underlying reasons, and the emotional toll it takes on the betrayed partner.

1.1 **Defining Infidelity under Types and Forms**

Infidelity manifests in different forms, ranging from physical affairs to emotional infidelity and even online relationships. Physical infidelity involves engaging in sexual activities with someone other than one's partner, while emotional infidelity encompasses forming strong emotional connections with individuals outside the relationship, often without physical intimacy. In today's digital age, the emergence of online infidelity, facilitated through social media platforms, dating apps, and online chat rooms, has added another layer of complexity to the dynamics of infidelity.

Moreover, infidelity can be categorized based on its duration and intensity. Some instances may involve one-time indiscretions, while others may evolve into long-term affairs. The level of secrecy and deception surrounding infidelity can also vary, with some individuals being upfront about their extramarital activities, while others go to great lengths to conceal them. Understanding these nuances is crucial in comprehending the multifaceted nature of infidelity and its impact on relationships.

1.2   **Exploring the Reasons Behind Infidelity**

The motivations behind infidelity are diverse and often deeply rooted in individual psychology and relational dynamics. While there is no one-size-fits-all explanation, several common factors contribute to the occurrence of infidelity. These include but are not limited to:

1. **Unmet Needs**: When one or both partners feel emotionally or physically neglected in the relationship, they may seek fulfillment elsewhere.

2. **Opportunity**: Opportunities for infidelity may arise in situations where individuals are exposed to new social circles, work environments, or online platforms that facilitate interactions with potential partners.

3. **Emotional Dissatisfaction**: Feelings of resentment, anger, or disillusionment within the relationship may drive individuals to seek validation, intimacy, or excitement outside the partnership.

4. **Personality Traits**: Certain personality traits, such as impulsivity, low self-control, or a propensity for risk-taking, can increase the likelihood of engaging in infidelity.

5. **Unresolved Issues**: Past traumas, unresolved conflicts, or unaddressed issues within the relationship can create vulnerabilities that make individuals more susceptible to infidelity.

Understanding these underlying reasons can provide insight into the dynamics at play within a relationship and inform efforts to address and prevent infidelity.

1.3 **Recognizing the Emotional Impact on the Betrayed Partner**

The emotional fallout of infidelity on the betrayed partner is profound and far-reaching. Betrayal trauma, characterized by feelings of shock, anger, disbelief, and profound sadness, can have devastating effects on an individual's mental and emotional well-being. The betrayed partner often experiences a profound loss of trust in both their partner and themselves, grappling with questions of self-worth, adequacy, and the viability of the relationship.

Furthermore, the aftermath of infidelity may trigger a range of psychological responses, including anxiety, depression, post-traumatic stress disorder (PTSD), and even suicidal ideation in severe cases. Rebuilding trust and repairing the relationship in the wake of infidelity requires a concerted effort from both partners, including open communication, empathy, accountability, and a willingness to address underlying issues.

In conclusion, understanding infidelity necessitates examining its various types, forms, underlying motivations, and the profound emotional impact it has on the betrayed partner. By recognizing the complexity of infidelity and its repercussions, individuals can work towards fostering healthier, more resilient relationships built on trust, communication, and mutual respect.

CHAPTER TWO

Coping with Betrayal

Betrayal inflicts a deep wound upon the soul, leaving individuals grappling with a complex array of emotions and questions. Whether the betrayal stems from infidelity, broken promises, or deceit, the aftermath can be overwhelming. Coping with betrayal requires navigating through the stages of grief, processing intense emotions, and seeking support from trusted sources. In this exploration, we delve into the various strategies for coping with betrayal and reclaiming a sense of stability and inner peace.

2.1   **Processing Shock and Disbelief under Betrayal**

The initial response to betrayal often involves shock and disbelief. The revelation of betrayal can shatter one's sense of reality, leaving them questioning the authenticity of their relationship and the motives of the betrayer. Processing this shock involves allowing oneself to acknowledge and validate their feelings of disbelief without judgment. It's essential to recognize that these reactions are natural responses to a profound breach of trust.

During this stage, individuals may experience a range of physical and emotional symptoms, including numbness, dissociation, and a sense of unreality. It's crucial to create a safe space for processing these feelings, whether through journaling, talking to a trusted friend, or seeking professional therapy. By acknowledging the reality of the betrayal and allowing oneself to experience the associated emotions, individuals can begin the healing process and move towards acceptance.

2.2 **Managing Intense Emotions: Anger, Hurt, and Sadness under Betrayal**

Anger, hurt, and sadness are common emotional responses to betrayal, each carrying its own unique challenges and complexities. Anger may manifest as a protective mechanism, shielding individuals from the pain of betrayal and providing a sense of empowerment in the face of vulnerability. However, unchecked anger can fuel resentment and perpetuate a cycle of negativity.

Hurt and sadness, on the other hand, stem from the profound sense of loss and betrayal experienced in the aftermath of betrayal. These emotions can be overwhelming, leading to feelings of despair, isolation, and self-doubt. Managing these intense emotions involves allowing oneself to grieve the loss of trust and the rupture of the relationship while also practicing self-compassion and forgiveness.

Engaging in self-care activities, such as exercise, mindfulness meditation, and creative expression, can provide outlets for processing and releasing pent-up emotions. Additionally, expressing feelings through healthy communication channels, such as assertive dialogue or writing letters (even if never sent), can facilitate emotional catharsis and promote healing.

2.3   **Seeking Support: Friends, Family, and Professionals**

Navigating the aftermath of betrayal can feel like an isolating journey, but no one has to endure it alone. Seeking support from friends, family, and mental health professionals can provide invaluable guidance, validation, and perspective during this challenging time. Friends and family members can offer unconditional love and empathy, serving as compassionate listeners and sources of emotional support.

Professional therapy, whether individual or couples counseling, can provide a structured environment for processing complex emotions, rebuilding trust, and developing healthier coping strategies.

Therapists offer impartial guidance and evidence-based techniques for managing stress, improving communication, and fostering resilience in the face of betrayal.

Moreover, support groups or online forums dedicated to individuals who have experienced betrayal can offer a sense of community and solidarity, reminding individuals that they are not alone in their struggles. By reaching out for support and allowing oneself to be vulnerable, individuals can cultivate a sense of hope and empowerment in the aftermath of betrayal.

In conclusion, coping with betrayal requires acknowledging and processing intense emotions, seeking support from trusted sources, and engaging in healthy coping mechanisms. While the journey towards healing may be arduous, it is ultimately a transformative process that can lead to greater self-awareness, resilience, and inner strength.

CHAPTER THREE

Rebuilding Trust under Infidelity

Infidelity strikes at the very core of a relationship, shattering trust and undermining the foundation upon which it was built. Rebuilding trust in the aftermath of infidelity is a challenging and often lengthy process that requires commitment, patience, and mutual effort from both partners. While the journey towards trust restoration may be fraught with obstacles, it is not insurmountable. In this exploration, we delve into the essential components of rebuilding trust after infidelity and the strategies for fostering healing and reconciliation.

3.1 **The Importance of Transparency and Honesty under Relationships**

Transparency and honesty are fundamental pillars of any healthy relationship, but they take on heightened significance in the aftermath of infidelity. Rebuilding trust requires a commitment to open communication and full disclosure from both partners. This entails being forthcoming about past indiscretions, feelings, and concerns, even when it may be uncomfortable or difficult.

Honesty is not only about revealing the truth but also about demonstrating integrity and consistency in one's words and actions. It involves being accountable for mistakes, showing genuine remorse, and actively working towards rebuilding trust through transparent behavior. Without honesty and transparency, trust cannot be restored, and the wounds of betrayal will continue to fester.

3.2   **Setting Boundaries and Expectations   under Relationships**

Setting clear boundaries and expectations is essential for establishing a sense of safety and predictability in the relationship. After infidelity, both partners may need to renegotiate their boundaries and redefine what is acceptable within the partnership. This process involves open dialogue, active listening, and a willingness to compromise.

Boundaries serve as guidelines for respectful behavior and help prevent future transgressions. They may include agreements about communication with members of the opposite sex, setting privacy boundaries regarding personal devices and social media accounts, and establishing protocols for rebuilding trust, such as regular check-ins and transparency measures.

Moreover, clarifying expectations ensures that both partners are on the same page regarding their needs, desires, and goals for the relationship moving forward. This may involve discussing the level of commitment, monogamy versus non-monogamy, and the steps each partner is willing to take to rebuild trust and strengthen the bond between them.

3.3 **Strategies for Restoring Trust in the Relationship**

Restoring trust after infidelity requires a multifaceted approach that addresses the emotional, psychological, and relational aspects of the betrayal. While there is no one-size-fits-all solution, several strategies can facilitate the healing process and promote reconciliation:

1. **Open Communication**: Foster honest and transparent communication by creating a safe space for both partners to express their feelings, concerns, and needs without fear of judgment or reprisal.

2. **Accountability**: The partner who engaged in infidelity must take full responsibility for their actions, demonstrate genuine remorse, and commit to making amends. This may involve seeking individual therapy, attending couples counseling, or participating in support groups for infidelity recovery.

3. **Rebuilding Intimacy**: Invest time and effort into rebuilding emotional and physical intimacy within the relationship. This may involve engaging in activities that foster connection, such as shared hobbies, date nights, and affectionate gestures.

4. **Consistency and Reliability**: Consistently demonstrate trustworthiness and reliability through actions that align with words. Follow through on commitments, honor agreements, and prioritize the well-being of the relationship above personal desires.

5. **Patience and Forgiveness**: Rebuilding trust takes time and patience. Both partners must be willing to forgive past transgressions and work towards a future based on mutual respect, understanding, and forgiveness.

In conclusion, rebuilding trust after infidelity is a challenging but achievable endeavor that requires honesty, transparency, and a commitment to open communication. By setting clear boundaries, managing expectations, and implementing strategies for restoring trust, couples can embark on a journey of healing and reconciliation, laying the groundwork for a stronger, more resilient relationship in the process.

CHAPTER FOUR

Communicating Effectively

Good communication is essential to a happy and successful relationship. It lays the foundation for understanding, trust, and intimacy between partners. Communicating effectively involves more than just exchanging words; it requires active listening, empathy, and the ability to express oneself honestly and respectfully. In this exploration, we delve into the essential components of effective communication in relationships, along with practical examples to illustrate its significance.

4.1 **Opening Up Dialogue About Feelings and Concerns**

Creating a culture of open dialogue about feelings and concerns is vital for fostering emotional intimacy and connection in a relationship. By encouraging vulnerability and authenticity, partners can deepen their understanding of each other's inner worlds and cultivate a sense of mutual support and empathy.

For example, instead of bottling up feelings of resentment or frustration, a partner might initiate a conversation by saying, "I've been feeling overlooked lately, and I'd like to talk to you about it." By expressing their emotions in a non-confrontational manner, they invite their partner to engage in a constructive dialogue and work towards resolution.

Similarly, discussing concerns or insecurities in a calm and non-judgmental manner can help alleviate misunderstandings and strengthen the bond between partners. For instance, expressing concerns about a partner's behavior or habits can be framed as an opportunity for mutual growth and understanding rather than criticism or blame.

4.2   **Active Listening and Validation**

Active listening is a fundamental skill that involves fully engaging with what the other person is saying, both verbally and non-verbally. It requires giving your full attention, maintaining eye contact, and refraining from interrupting or formulating a response prematurely. Active listening also involves validating the other person's emotions and experiences, even if you may not agree with their perspective.

For example, if a partner expresses feelings of insecurity about their career, active listening involves paraphrasing their concerns and reflecting them back, such as saying, "It sounds like you're feeling uncertain about your career path right now." This demonstrates empathy and validation, fostering a sense of connection and understanding.

Additionally, validating a partner's emotions does not necessarily mean agreeing with their viewpoint but rather acknowledging the validity of their feelings and experiences. By affirming their emotions and providing a supportive presence, partners can create a safe space for open communication and vulnerability.

4.3 **Resolving Conflict Constructively**

Conflict is an inevitable part of any relationship, but how it is managed can make a significant difference in its outcome. Resolving conflict constructively involves approaching disagreements with a spirit of collaboration, empathy, and respect for each other's perspectives. It requires effective communication skills, a willingness to compromise, and a commitment to finding mutually satisfactory solutions.

One constructive approach to resolving conflict is the use of "I" statements to express thoughts and feelings without assigning blame. For example, instead of saying, "You never listen to me," a partner might say, "I feel unheard when I don't get a chance to share my perspective."

Moreover, practicing active problem-solving techniques, such as brainstorming possible solutions together and evaluating their feasibility, can help partners work towards resolution in a collaborative manner. It's also essential to take breaks when emotions are running high and revisit the conversation when both partners are in a calmer state of mind.

Furthermore, prioritizing the relationship over being right and seeking common ground can facilitate compromise and reconciliation. By focusing on understanding each other's needs and finding win-win solutions, partners can emerge from conflict with a deeper sense of connection and mutual respect.

To sum up, having good communication is crucial to fostering happy, fulfilling relationships. By opening up dialogue about feelings and concerns, practicing active listening and validation, and resolving conflict constructively, partners can cultivate a strong foundation of trust, intimacy, and understanding, paving the way for a lasting and harmonious relationship.

CHAPTER FIVE

Forgiveness and Moving Forward

Forgiveness is a powerful yet challenging aspect of healing in the aftermath of infidelity. It involves letting go of resentment and anger towards the betraying partner and choosing to move forward with a sense of compassion and understanding. While forgiveness does not condone or excuse the actions of the betrayer, it frees the betrayed partner from the burden of carrying emotional pain and allows them to reclaim their sense of peace and well-being. In this exploration, we delve into the complexities of forgiveness in infidelity relationships, along with practical examples illustrating its transformative impact.

5.1 **Understanding the Process of Forgiveness**

Forgiveness is not a one-time event but rather a gradual and often nonlinear process that unfolds over time. It involves acknowledging and processing the pain caused by the betrayal, accepting the reality of what happened, and choosing to release the emotional baggage associated with it. The journey towards forgiveness may involve various stages, including:

1. **Acknowledgment**:The betrayed partner acknowledges the hurt and betrayal they experienced, allowing themselves to fully feel and express their emotions without judgment.

2. **Empathy**: Developing empathy towards the betraying partner involves recognizing their humanity and understanding the factors that may have contributed to their actions, such as unmet needs or unresolved issues.

3. **Decision**: Forgiveness is ultimately a choice, and the betrayed partner must actively decide to let go of resentment and anger towards the betraying partner. This decision may be facilitated by a desire to heal and move forward with their life.

4. **Healing**: Forgiveness is intrinsically linked to the healing process, as it allows the betrayed partner to release emotional pain and reclaim their sense of inner peace and well-being.

5. **Reconciliation (optional)**: While forgiveness is separate from reconciliation, some couples may choose to work towards rebuilding their relationship after infidelity. However, reconciliation should only be pursued if both partners are willing to engage in

honest communication, trust-building efforts, and professional support.

5.2   **Letting Go of Resentment and Bitterness**

Resentment and bitterness are natural responses to betrayal, but holding onto these emotions only prolongs the suffering of the betrayed partner. Letting go of resentment involves releasing the desire for revenge or retribution and instead focusing on personal healing and growth. It requires reframing the narrative of the betrayal from one of victimhood to one of empowerment and resilience.

For example, instead of harboring resentment towards the betraying partner, the betrayed partner may choose to view the experience as an opportunity for self-discovery and growth. They may channel their energy into activities that promote self-care, personal development, and rebuilding their sense of self-worth.

Moreover, forgiveness does not mean forgetting or condoning the betrayal but rather choosing to no longer let it define or control one's life. By releasing resentment and bitterness, the betrayed partner creates space for positive emotions such as compassion, empathy, and inner peace to flourish.

5.3   **Embracing Healing and Growth Opportunities**

Infidelity, while deeply painful, can also serve as a catalyst for profound healing and growth. Embracing healing and growth opportunities involves acknowledging the lessons learned from the experience, fostering self-awareness, and embracing the possibility of positive transformation.

For instance, the betrayed partner may discover newfound resilience and inner strength as they navigate the challenges of rebuilding trust and moving forward with their life. They may also gain a deeper understanding of their needs, boundaries, and values, which can inform future relationship dynamics.

Additionally, seeking professional therapy or support groups can provide valuable guidance and support on the journey towards healing and growth. Therapists can offer tools and techniques for processing emotions, rebuilding self-esteem, and cultivating healthier relationship patterns.

Furthermore, infidelity can prompt couples to reassess and strengthen their relationship, leading to greater intimacy, trust, and connection. By engaging in open and honest communication, practicing empathy and forgiveness, and prioritizing mutual growth and well-being, couples can emerge from the experience with a renewed sense of commitment and resilience.

In conclusion, forgiveness and moving forward after infidelity require courage, compassion, and a willingness to embrace healing and growth opportunities. By understanding the process of forgiveness, letting go of resentment and bitterness, and embracing the possibility of positive transformation, individuals can reclaim their sense of self-worth, inner peace, and capacity for love and trust in future relationships.

CHAPTER SIX

Reconnecting Intimately After Infidelity in Relationships

Infidelity can shatter the trust and intimacy in a relationship, leaving both partners feeling wounded, betrayed, and disconnected. However, it is possible to rebuild and reconnect intimately after such a breach of trust. Rebuilding emotional intimacy, restoring physical intimacy and affection, and overcoming the challenges and barriers to reconnection require patience, understanding, and commitment from both parties involved.

6.1   **Rebuilding Emotional Intimacy**

Rebuilding emotional intimacy after infidelity is a complex and challenging process that requires open communication, vulnerability, and a willingness to address the underlying issues that led to the betrayal. Both partners need to be willing to engage in honest conversations about their feelings, fears, and insecurities. This may involve seeking couples therapy or counseling to navigate through the emotional turmoil and rebuild trust.

One effective strategy for rebuilding emotional intimacy is practicing empathy and active listening. Each partner needs to feel heard and understood without judgment or defensiveness. This involves validating each other's feelings, expressing remorse for the hurt caused, and demonstrating a sincere commitment to change and growth.

Another crucial aspect of rebuilding emotional intimacy is forgiveness. Forgiveness is not about condoning the betrayal but rather letting go of the resentment and anger that can poison the relationship. It requires a willingness to heal and move forward together, acknowledging that rebuilding trust takes time and effort.

Additionally, couples can benefit from reconnecting through shared activities and experiences that foster emotional closeness. This could include going on dates, taking up a new hobby together, or participating in couples' retreats or workshops focused on rebuilding trust and intimacy.

6.2   **Restoring Physical Intimacy and Affection**

Restoring physical intimacy and affection after infidelity can be particularly challenging due to the breach of trust and emotional pain involved. However, it is essential to recognize that physical intimacy is an integral part of a healthy relationship and can play a crucial role in reconnecting with your partner.

One approach to restoring physical intimacy is to start slowly and gradually reintroduce physical touch and affection into the relationship. This could involve simple gestures such as holding hands, hugging, or cuddling without the expectation of immediate sexual intimacy. Building trust and emotional intimacy is essential before diving back into a sexual relationship.

Communication is key when it comes to restoring physical intimacy. Both partners need to feel comfortable expressing their desires, boundaries, and concerns regarding physical intimacy. This may involve discussing any lingering feelings of insecurity or fear of further betrayal and working together to address them in a supportive and understanding manner.

Seeking professional help from a therapist or sex therapist can also be beneficial for couples struggling to restore physical intimacy after infidelity. A trained therapist can provide guidance, support, and practical techniques for reconnecting intimately and rebuilding trust in the relationship.

6.3   **Overcoming Challenges and Barriers to Reconnection**

Overcoming the challenges and barriers to reconnection after infidelity requires a concerted effort from both partners and a commitment to healing and rebuilding the relationship. One of the most significant barriers to reconnection is the presence of unresolved issues and lingering resentment from the infidelity.

To overcome these challenges, both partners need to be willing to confront the underlying issues that contributed to the infidelity and work together to address them. This may involve seeking individual therapy to explore personal issues such as low self-esteem, communication problems, or unresolved trauma that may have contributed to the betrayal.

Another common barrier to reconnection is a lack of trust. Rebuilding trust takes time and consistency, and both partners need to demonstrate honesty, reliability, and transparency in their words and actions. This may involve setting boundaries, being accountable for their behavior, and being patient with each other's healing process.

Couples may also face external challenges such as judgment or criticism from friends and family, which can further strain the relationship. It is essential to prioritize the needs of the relationship and establish boundaries with outside influences that may undermine the reconnection process.

Ultimately, overcoming the challenges and barriers to reconnection after infidelity requires patience, understanding, and a shared commitment to healing and rebuilding the relationship. It is not an easy journey, but with dedication and support, couples can emerge stronger and more connected than ever before.

CHAPTER SEVEN

Addressing Underlying Issues Under Infidelity Relationships

Addressing underlying issues is essential for healing and rebuilding trust in a relationship after infidelity. These issues can range from communication breakdowns to unresolved personal traumas. By addressing these underlying issues, couples can create a foundation for a healthier and more resilient relationship moving forward.

One common underlying issue that can contribute to infidelity is a lack of communication. When partners feel unable to express their needs, desires, or concerns openly and honestly, they may seek emotional or physical intimacy outside of the relationship. For example, if one partner feels neglected or unappreciated, they may turn to someone else for validation and attention.

Another underlying issue that can contribute to infidelity is unresolved conflict or resentment. When conflicts are left unaddressed or unresolved, they can build up over time and create distance between partners. This can lead to feelings of anger, frustration, or resentment, which may drive one partner to seek solace or validation elsewhere.

Additionally, underlying issues such as stress, financial strain, or life transitions can put a strain on a relationship and increase the likelihood of infidelity. For example, if a couple is experiencing financial difficulties or struggling with work-life balance, they may feel disconnected from each other and more susceptible to seeking comfort outside of the relationship.

7.1 **Exploring Contributing Factors: Stress, Communication, etc.**

Exploring contributing factors to infidelity is crucial for understanding why it occurred and how to prevent it in the future. Stress is one of the most significant contributing factors to infidelity, as it can impair judgment, increase emotional vulnerability, and lead to poor decision-making. When individuals are under high levels of stress, they may be more likely to seek out temporary relief or distraction in the form of an affair.

Communication breakdowns are another common contributing factor to infidelity. When partners feel unable to communicate openly and honestly with each other, they may turn to someone else to fulfill their emotional or physical needs. This can lead to a breakdown in trust and intimacy within the relationship.

Other contributing factors to infidelity may include unresolved personal issues such as low self-esteem, past trauma, or a history of infidelity in previous relationships. These underlying issues can create vulnerabilities that make individuals more susceptible to engaging in extramarital affairs.

7.2   **Healing Past Wounds and Trauma**

Healing past wounds and trauma is essential for creating a strong and resilient relationship. Past traumas such as childhood abuse, abandonment, or betrayal can have a profound impact on an individual's ability to trust and connect with others. When these wounds are left unaddressed, they can manifest in dysfunctional patterns of behavior, including infidelity.

One approach to healing past wounds and trauma is individual therapy or counseling. A trained therapist can provide a safe and supportive environment for individuals to explore their past experiences, identify how they have been affected by them, and develop healthy coping mechanisms for moving forward.

Couples therapy or counseling can also be beneficial for addressing past wounds and trauma within the context of the relationship. A skilled therapist can help couples communicate more effectively, develop empathy and understanding for each other's experiences, and work through any unresolved conflicts or resentments that may be contributing to the infidelity.

In addition to therapy, self-care practices such as mindfulness, meditation, and self-reflection can help individuals heal from past wounds and trauma. By cultivating self-awareness and self-compassion, individuals can learn to recognize and address the ways in which their past experiences may be impacting their current relationships.

7.3   **Seeking Professional Help: Therapy and Counseling**

Seeking professional help through therapy and counseling is essential for couples navigating the aftermath of infidelity. Infidelity can create deep emotional wounds and fractures in a relationship that may be challenging to heal on their own. A qualified therapist can offer direction, encouragement, and useful tools to help the couple restore intimacy, communication, and trust.

Individual therapy can be beneficial for both partners to explore their own feelings, motivations, and underlying issues related to infidelity. This can help individuals gain insight into their own behavior, patterns, and triggers, and develop healthier ways of relating to themselves and their partners.

Couples therapy or counseling is also crucial for addressing the impact of infidelity on the relationship as a whole. A skilled therapist can facilitate open and honest communication between partners, help them navigate through feelings of anger, betrayal, and hurt, and work together to rebuild trust and intimacy.

In addition to traditional therapy, there are also specialized programs and workshops available for couples dealing with infidelity. These programs often focus on rebuilding trust, improving communication, and strengthening the emotional connection between partners. By investing in professional help, couples can increase their chances of healing and rebuilding their relationship after infidelity.

CHAPTER EIGHT

Strengthening the Relationship

Strengthening a relationship after infidelity requires intentional effort and commitment from both partners. It involves rebuilding trust, communication, and intimacy while addressing underlying issues that contributed to the betrayal. By focusing on strengthening the relationship, couples can create a solid foundation for long-term happiness and fulfillment.

One essential aspect of strengthening the relationship is cultivating friendship and mutual respect. Friendship forms the basis of a healthy relationship, providing a sense of camaraderie, companionship, and emotional support. By prioritizing friendship, couples can create a strong bond built on trust, loyalty, and shared values.

Another key component of strengthening the relationship is fostering a culture of appreciation and gratitude. Expressing appreciation for each other's efforts, qualities, and contributions helps reinforce positive feelings and deepen emotional connection. Regular expressions of gratitude can strengthen the bond between partners and create a more positive and supportive relationship environment.

8.1 **Cultivating Friendship and Mutual Respect**

Cultivating friendship and mutual respect is essential for creating a strong and resilient relationship. Friendship involves enjoying each other's company, sharing common interests, and being there for each other through thick and thin. When couples prioritize friendship, they create a solid foundation for trust, communication, and intimacy.

One way to cultivate friendship in a relationship is by spending quality time together doing activities that both partners enjoy. This could include hobbies, interests, or shared experiences that bring joy and fulfillment to both individuals. By nurturing shared interests and creating new memories together, couples can strengthen their bond and deepen their friendship.

Mutual respect is another critical aspect of a healthy relationship. It involves treating each other with kindness, empathy, and consideration, even during times of conflict or disagreement. When partners respect each other's boundaries, opinions, and autonomy, they create a safe and supportive relationship environment where both individuals feel valued and appreciated.

8.2 **Fostering a Culture of Appreciation and Gratitude**

Fostering a culture of appreciation and gratitude is essential for nurturing a positive and fulfilling relationship. Expressing gratitude for each other's actions, qualities, and efforts helps reinforce positive behavior and strengthen emotional connection. By cultivating a habit of appreciation, couples can create a more supportive and loving relationship environment.

One way to foster a culture of appreciation is by regularly expressing gratitude for the little things that partners do for each other. This could include thanking each other for acts of kindness, words of encouragement, or gestures of love and affection. By acknowledging and appreciating each other's efforts, couples can reinforce positive behavior and deepen their emotional bond.

Another way to foster appreciation and gratitude is by practicing acts of kindness and generosity towards each other. This could involve surprising your partner with thoughtful gifts, acts of service, or words of affirmation that show your love and appreciation. By making an effort to make each other feel valued and cherished, couples can create a more loving and supportive relationship dynamic.

8.3 **Investing in the Relationship: Quality Time and Shared Goals**

Investing in the relationship is essential for fostering long-term happiness and fulfillment. This involves prioritizing quality time together and working towards shared goals and aspirations. By investing time and energy into the relationship, couples can create a strong foundation for growth, intimacy, and mutual fulfillment.

Quality time is essential for building intimacy and connection in a relationship. This could involve spending time together without distractions, such as going on date nights, taking walks, or having meaningful conversations. By making time for each other and nurturing emotional connection, couples can strengthen their bond and deepen their love for each other.

Shared goals and aspirations provide a sense of purpose and direction in a relationship. By working towards common objectives, couples can foster a sense of teamwork, collaboration, and mutual support. Whether it's saving for a dream vacation, starting a family, or pursuing personal passions together, shared goals can strengthen the bond between partners and create a deeper sense of unity and partnership.

In brief, strengthening a relationship after infidelity requires intentional effort and commitment from both partners. By cultivating friendship and mutual respect, fostering a culture of appreciation and gratitude, and investing in quality time and shared goals, couples can create a strong and resilient relationship built on trust, communication, and love.

CHAPTER NINE

Managing Triggers and Relapses

Managing triggers and relapses is crucial for individuals and couples navigating the aftermath of infidelity. Triggers are events, situations, or stimuli that reignite painful emotions or memories associated with the betrayal, while relapses refer to setbacks or moments of regression in the healing process. By learning to manage triggers and navigate relapses effectively, individuals and couples can strengthen their resilience and continue on the path towards healing and rebuilding their relationship.

9.1 **Identifying Triggers That Reignite Pain and Doubt**

Identifying triggers that reignite pain and doubt is the first step in managing them effectively. Triggers can vary widely from person to person and may include anything from specific locations or activities to certain words or phrases. Common triggers for individuals who have experienced infidelity may include seeing a particular restaurant where the affair took place, hearing a song that reminds them of the betrayal, or encountering a social media post that triggers feelings of jealousy or insecurity.

9.2 **Developing Coping Strategies and Self-Care Practices**

Developing coping strategies and self-care practices is essential for managing triggers and navigating relapses in the aftermath of infidelity. Coping strategies can include both practical techniques for managing difficult emotions in the moment and proactive measures for maintaining emotional well-being over the long term. Self-care practices are activities or rituals that promote physical, emotional, and mental well-being and can help individuals build resilience and cope with stress.

One effective coping strategy for managing triggers is mindfulness meditation. Being mindful entails paying attention to one's thoughts and feelings while stepping back from judgment. By practicing mindfulness meditation regularly, individuals can learn to identify triggers as they arise and respond to them in a calm and grounded manner.

Another coping strategy is seeking support from trusted friends, family members, or support groups. Talking openly about triggers and relapses with supportive individuals can help individuals feel less alone and more understood. Support groups specifically for individuals who have experienced infidelity can provide a safe space for sharing experiences, exchanging coping strategies, and receiving validation and encouragement from others who have been through similar challenges.

In addition to coping strategies, self-care practices play a vital role in managing triggers and navigating relapses. Self-care activities can include exercise, healthy eating, getting enough sleep, spending time in nature, engaging in hobbies or creative pursuits, and practicing relaxation techniques such as deep breathing or progressive muscle relaxation. Taking care of oneself physically, emotionally, and mentally is essential for building resilience and coping effectively with the ups and downs of the healing journey.

9.3   **Reaffirming Commitment and Resilience in the Face of Setbacks**

Reaffirming commitment and resilience in the face of setbacks is essential for individuals and couples navigating the challenges of healing from infidelity. Setbacks are a natural part of the healing process and may include relapses, conflicts, or moments of doubt. By reaffirming their commitment to each other and drawing on their resilience, couples can overcome setbacks and continue moving forward on the path towards healing and reconciliation.

One way to reaffirm commitment in the face of setbacks is by openly communicating with each other about feelings, needs, and concerns. Couples can use setbacks as an opportunity to deepen their understanding of each other and strengthen their bond. By talking honestly and compassionately about what triggered the setback and how it made each partner feel, couples can work together to address underlying issues and find solutions.

Another way to reaffirm commitment is by focusing on the positive aspects of the relationship and the progress that has been made. Celebrating milestones, no matter how small, can help couples stay motivated and hopeful during difficult times. By acknowledging the hard work and dedication that each partner has put into the healing process, couples can reaffirm their commitment to each other and their shared goals for the future.

Drawing on resilience is essential for navigating setbacks and overcoming challenges in the healing journey. Resilience is the ability to bounce back from adversity and continue moving forward in the face of obstacles. Couples can strengthen their resilience by cultivating a growth mindset, practicing self-compassion, and drawing on their support networks for encouragement and guidance.

In conclusion, managing triggers and relapses, identifying triggers that reignite pain and doubt, developing coping strategies and self-care practices, and reaffirming commitment and resilience in the face of setbacks are essential components of the healing journey after infidelity. By learning to manage triggers effectively, individuals and couples can navigate relapses with grace and resilience, reaffirming their commitment to each other and their shared goals for the future.

CHAPTER TEN

Embracing a New Beginning After the Phase of Infidelity in Relationship

Embracing a new beginning after experiencing infidelity in a relationship or marriage can be a daunting but transformative journey. It marks a pivotal moment where individuals and couples have the opportunity to reassess their values, priorities, and aspirations for the future. While the pain and betrayal of infidelity may cast a shadow, it also presents an opportunity for growth, healing, and renewal.

To embrace a new beginning, individuals and couples must first acknowledge and process the emotions that accompany the discovery or disclosure of infidelity. It is natural to feel a range of emotions, including shock, anger, sadness, and betrayal. It is essential to allow oneself to feel these emotions fully and to seek support from trusted friends, family members, or professionals if needed.

As individuals begin to navigate the aftermath of infidelity, they may find themselves questioning their identity and self-worth. The experience of betrayal can shake one's sense of self and leave them feeling lost or inadequate. However, reclaiming personal identity and confidence is a crucial step towards healing and moving forward.

10.1 **Reclaiming Personal Identity and Confidence**

Reclaiming personal identity and confidence after experiencing infidelity involves reconnecting with one's values, passions, and strengths. It requires individuals to reflect on who they are outside of their relationship and to rediscover the things that bring them joy and fulfillment. This may involve pursuing hobbies, interests, or goals that have been neglected or forgotten during the tumultuous period of infidelity.

Additionally, reclaiming personal identity and confidence requires individuals to challenge negative beliefs and narratives that may have emerged as a result of the betrayal. It is common for individuals who have experienced infidelity to internalize feelings of inadequacy, unworthiness, or blame. However, it is essential to recognize that one's worth and value are not defined by the actions of others, and to practice self-compassion and self-care.

Building a support network of friends, family members, or support groups can also be instrumental in reclaiming personal identity and confidence. Surrounding oneself with positive and supportive individuals who affirm and validate one's worth can help counteract negative self-talk and boost self-esteem.

10.2   **Building a Shared Vision for the Future**

Building a shared vision for the future is essential for couples navigating the aftermath of infidelity. While the betrayal may have caused a rupture in trust and intimacy, it also presents an opportunity for couples to redefine their relationship and create a new narrative moving forward. Building a shared vision requires open and honest communication, vulnerability, and a willingness to dream and plan together.

Couples can start by reflecting on their individual values, goals, and aspirations for the future and identifying areas of alignment and shared purpose. This may involve discussing topics such as career ambitions, family planning, lifestyle preferences, and personal growth objectives. By openly communicating about their hopes, dreams, and fears, couples can deepen their understanding of each other and create a roadmap for the future.

10.3   **Celebrating Milestones and Achievements in the Healing Journey***

Celebrating milestones and achievements in the healing journey of infidelity is essential for acknowledging progress, fostering positivity, and reinforcing commitment. Healing from infidelity is not a linear process, and it is essential to recognize and celebrate the small victories along the way. Whether it's reaching a milestone in therapy, having a difficult conversation with honesty and compassion, or experiencing moments of joy and connection, each achievement deserves to be acknowledged and celebrated.

10.4 **Questions and Discussion under Healing from Infidelity**

Q: How can couples rebuild trust after infidelity?

A: Rebuilding trust after infidelity requires open communication, honesty, and consistency. Both partners need to be willing to address the underlying issues that led to the betrayal, and demonstrate a sincere commitment to change and growth. This may involve seeking couples therapy or counseling to navigate through the emotional turmoil and rebuild trust.

Q: Is it possible to forgive after infidelity?

A: Forgiveness is a complex and deeply personal process that varies from person to person. While forgiveness may not happen overnight, it is possible with time, effort, and a willingness to let go of resentment and anger. Forgiveness does not mean condoning the betrayal, but rather releasing the emotional burden and moving forward with a sense of peace and closure.

Q: How can individuals rebuild their self-esteem after infidelity?

A: Rebuilding self-esteem after infidelity involves reconnecting with one's values, passions, and strengths, and practicing self-compassion and self-care. This may involve seeking support from friends, family, or a therapist, and engaging in activities that bring joy and fulfillment. It's essential to remember that self-esteem is a journey, and it's okay to seek help and support along the way.

Q: What role does communication play in healing from infidelity?

A: Communication plays a central role in healing from infidelity, as it allows couples to express their feelings, needs, and concerns openly and honestly. Effective communication involves active listening, empathy, and a willingness to engage in difficult conversations with honesty and compassion. By communicating openly and authentically, couples can address underlying issues, rebuild trust, and strengthen their bond.

Q: How can couples navigate triggers and setbacks in the healing journey?

A: Navigating triggers and setbacks in the healing journey requires self-awareness, patience, and resilience. Couples can identify triggers that reignite painful emotions or memories and develop coping strategies and self-care practices to manage them effectively. It's essential to reaffirm commitment to each other and draw on resilience in the face of setbacks, and celebrate milestones and achievements along the way.